My Pelvis Wants to Be Elvis

Nolcha Fox

Acknowledgments

This book contains my favorite poems I've written since *Memory is that raccoon.*

Thanks to the many literary magazine editors and to My Bad Poetry podcasters for graciously giving my poems a home. And for their sense of humor (they've needed it). I acknowledge them at the end of each poem.

Thanks to Dr. Karunesh for nudging me to put this book together.

Thanks to my mother, who loved me before I was born. She always applauds everything I write.

A special thanks to my husband, whom I love dearly. He's held my hand for the past 25 years so that I won't fly away.

Contents

Knife

Time is a surgeon who flunked medical school.
He operates with imprecision,
cutting away the fat of the day,
slashing through the hours with a pocket knife.
When Time is finished, there is
nothing left of me. Even my bones are
nothing but dust.

(Published in Hotel Masticadores)

Impossible Landscapes

You flicker, a warmth
lighting corners in shadows,
still bright, even though
you are years from this house.
The silk scarf haphazardly
tossed on the armchair,
your fragrance, your heat
even now leaves me dizzy,
though silk scarf and armchair
are antiques long gone.
Your smile painted landscapes
I store in the attic,
believing they'll call you
and bring you back home.

(Published in The Wind Phone)

Boardwalk Fabric

Skaters, joggers, bicyclists, walkers
weave in and out, practiced
at seeing but not seeing.
A brush of skin floats in the breeze,
a needle in the fabric of obscurity.
Random colors bleed in motion,
smiles pasted to the fibers
of this summer day.

Blame the Cat

Who else could teach our bicycles to roll up that big tree,
and hang their wheels below the leaves for everyone to see?
Who else could teach the wintering deer to clamber up the roof
for selfie opportunities to send to friends as proof?
We have to blame the cat because he doesn't give a crap,
and flicks his tail erratically while settling in to nap.

(Published in MuddyUm)

I am a settler settling

in the present tense, my past tense
is my luggage that retired to somewhere else.
I eat canned food with plastic spoons
I stored for this world's end
that starts again each morning
when I roll up my bed.

(Published in Medusa's Kitchen)

Drunk

Be the ants upon the log, barely sober.
Nothing wrong with hot mulled cider.
Square dance on a piano
played by tigers chasing chickens.
Dip pirate hats in queso, snarling *Aarrgh*.
Ask us any question, we act stupid.
We are punch-drunk lumberjacks
concealing love notes pressed in comics.
It's September, eat a hoagie,
toss the clock out, no one cares if we are late,
we are ok, we lick iguanas, never mind
that's pretty awful, ride an ampersand
and don't forget dessert, buy two for one.

(Published in MuddyUm)

Tailgate

The hours crowd, they tailgate,
they long to reach their journey's end.
Perhaps they think of party time,
to share some beers beneath the stars.
Give me some room, don't make me rush,
I'll reach oblivion all by myself.

Lean

Memories are the leaves
of your messy life,
pierced by aphids
and sunlight,
parasailing with the wind,
landing in gutters
that dim with age,
crinkling underfoot,
sticking to your shoes,
crushed into different stories.
Lean against the tree.
Shake it.

Line

Not drunk, he walked between the spaces, spaces where the faded yellow line would stutter, change its mind, begin its job of separating bad from good, from here and there. No cop could stop the fault he felt was his, a fault, a quake that waved the faded yellow line, he thought it drunk the way it wavered down the road that stopped at nowhere good, that faded yellow into good intentions gone the wrong side of the empty road.

(Published by Roi Faineant Press)

Don't Dwell

Bought and sold, and bought again,
we catch and cage our flighty souls,
then barter them for useless things.
They long to soar where we can't see,
but fade in gold captivity.
Now we are void of currency.
Don't dwell on what has passed away.

First and last lines from Leonard Cohen's "Anthem"

(Published on Medium)

Living in Time

I bought this jacket at the corner of here and there, from a shop between then and maybe. A thread unravels from the sleeve into a now that pokes a disremembered hole in my pocket. The hole leaks change that rolls behind my squeaky shoes. I should oil them. Fry them. Filet of sole. I have a ticket to a time I haven't heard of, a place that isn't there, then, or maybe. Maybe I shouldn't go.

Water

He was a torrent,
a deluge,
a downpour,
a wall of water,
a waterfall,
unstoppable,
untamable.
He swept her away,
pulled her under.
He was a force
that left her breathless.
He tossed her aside,
a shipwrecked distress.
She clung to the driftwood
of mourning.

(Accepted for publication in December 2023 Alien Buddha Zine)

Ugh

Each scratchy sheet
a blanket to blow in,
a sampler of sneezes
and watery eyes.
The box is now empty,
I fill it with wadded
and snotty reminders,
a nest for a birdbrain
who left windows open,
and woke up to
headache and chest cold
and stuffed nose
and pain.

(Accepted for publication in December 2023 Alien Buddha Zine)

Deadbeat

Her shadow was a lazy loafer,
hiding in the corners of the rooms.
It ate the dog food,
spilled the tea,
left a trail of pizza crusts.
Her shadow mooched
on midnight moans,
borrowed spare change
from the coin jar,
stole the sunshine
from the porch.
Her shadow didn't want to leave,
although its body shoved off
with a suitcase years ago.

(Published in Dark Entries)

Miracle in Glass

So often we have knocked you off
your stand, we've dropped you on your drerp,
yet you refuse to break.
You endure such bitter brew
that melts our spoons
and curls our teeth.
You've stood unwashed
for days on end,
and still you don't complain.
I hope you haunt
this hopeless house
since your design
is out of stock.
We need you, coffee pot.

(Published on Medium)

Dangerous Curves Ahead

Your dress reveals your buxom breasts,
your rounded hips, your luscious legs.
Your feet arch high in spike and spite heels.
You're a barrel of regrets on a runaway train,
and all your signals are broken.

(Published in Contemplate)

What He Is

He is a sonic boom
wrinkling my walls.
He is a disco ball
reflecting the sun.
He is a bullet
searching for the sky.
He is an oil slick
evading the record of his misdeeds.

Thanks to Carly M Cherry's poem, "They Tried to Race the Moon" for some of the words and images I used.

(Published in Micropoetry Cosmos)

Home Invasion

Yesterday holds a gun to my head,
demands wasted time in nickels and quarters.

Today holds the bullets, collects empty cartridges.
You're so disappointing, he says.

Tomorrow tip-toes to the door.
He wants to leave before the bleeding starts.

(Published in Five Fleas)

Summer Slips

Red slips, a slinker,
tipping tiptoe on the leaves.
It strangles sun, it oozes blood,
as warm days crinkle yellow.
A final grasp, a breath of wind
 to gasp and rasp of autumn.
I turn around, the leaves fall down
as summer slips away.

(Published in Medusa's Kitchen)

Inside Myself

I stood inside myself
to hide from hammers banging nails
deep inside my head.
A fractured line of bone and blood
that ran from past to future,
escape obscured by blinding lights
that punctured every thought.
Words were cannons shots,
gun powder blasting through
my shield of self-defense.
I crumbled and dissolved
into an oil spill, eating earth
until the grass turned black.

First and last lines from Gregory Orr's "Self-Portrait at Twenty"

(Published in Garden of Neuro)

Reflection on Priorities

He stopped in front of every storefront
that reflected back his clone.
He checked and combed his hair
so every curl was in its place.
He checked his teeth for spinach,
then rustled up his sleeve to flex
his bicep and impress the girl

who walked away a block ago.

(Published in Doctor Funny)

Velveteen Waiting

The blue velveteen chair
by the window knows
how to wait.
The blue velveteen chair
waits for the curtains to open,
for the sun to lay itself
across soft blue arms.
The blue velveteen chair
waits for the dog
to fall asleep on its lap.
The blue velveteen chair
waits for the curtains to close,
for the lights to turn on.
The blue velveteen chair
knows how to fill up the corner
with patience.

(Published in Contemplate)

Upright

His back a board, he leans at waist,
to scrutinize the keys.
His eyebrows meet, two shaggy mutts,
to contemplate a feast
of music not yet brought to sound.
His ears aflutter, fingers raised
to dance on blacks and whites,
the piano tuner takes a breath
before he starts to work.

(Published in Medusa's Kitchen)

We didn't know

what we would find,
when you left us forever.
We came together
to clean up, clean out.
We didn't know
the depths of pretense,
the sham of family love.
We didn't know
how broken we were
until you broke us.

(Published in Put It To Rest)

Sparklies

I hold a sparkler in my hand
to add to my collection
of shiny things that grab my eye
and mess with my attention.
Shiny shells and shiny stones
and sun and wind and moon,
even if it doesn't move
my thoughts are sure to follow.

(Published on Medium)

If Hemingway wrote

a manual for my slow cooker,
it would read,
ordcr in tonight.

(Published in Doctor Funny)

Undiscovered

I find myself in wilderness I never thought I'd see.
Rolling hills and prickly fields in hues of brown and gray,
a place where time has not caught up to what I used to be.
The ground is strewn with mirrors that are cracked and warped
and cloudy.
Looking down I see me older, undiscovered territory.

(Published in Mad Swirl)

Second Cup

I poured myself a second cup
at 8 o'clock this morning.
I need caffeine
but interruptions
keep me from partaking.
It's cold again,
the cream congealed.
What a yucky sight.
I bought a cup
a block away,
and now I hope
to drink it up
before I go to bed.

(Published in Doctor Funny, republished in Fine Lines)

Entertainment Police

They knock on my door at midnight,
flashing badges and ultra-white teeth.
You haven't met your quota
of daily dribble, they say.
Where is your TV?
I don't have one, I say.
Just as we suspected.
They crack open my head.
Here's the problem. they say,
She's a starfish in a sky of stars.

(Published in Spread, republished on Medium)

Here and Out of Reach

Morning landed with a thud
and skidded down the roof.
I stuck my cup outside with hopes
that I could catch and drink it.
But Morning was a trickster
and bounced into a tree.
I'll never get my morning fix
when it is out of reach.

(Published in Contemplate)

If sleep was an elevator

I would be stuck between floors,
pressing all the buttons,
calling for help. But help never comes.
I crawl out somehow, isn't it a dream?
Or a nightmare?
The emergency lights in the halls
I wander, flicker, strobe.
the doors are all locked,
no doorknobs, I pound them,
they're rubber.

If sleep was an elevator,
I'd take the stairs.

(Published in Lothlorien Poetry Journal)

Storm

Slickers are windows for raindrops to
slide down to kneecaps and
seep through my jeans.
Slipping and
splashing, I
stomp into
puddles. I'm
soaked by the time I get home.

(Published in Lothlorien Poetry Journal)

Good Intentions

I intended to rest on Sunday.
But I was busy worrying
about everything I couldn't do.
Laundry. Pulling weeds.
Food shopping. Picking up stamps.

I intended to do on Monday
what I didn't do on Sunday.
But I was so tired from
being busy worrying,
I slept through most of Monday.

I intended to remember on Tuesday
what I had to do on Sunday
that I didn't do on Monday.

I forgot what I intended to do.

(Published in MuddyUm)

I Can Lose Anything

I've lost my keys.
I've lost my hat.
I've lost myself in thought.
I've lost my wallet.
I've lost my mind.
I've even lost the dog.
I'll probably be
the one to lose

the nametag on my toe.

(Published in MuddyUm)

Quacks

I wonder if my row of ducks
is really made of ducks at all.
One prefers a garbage bin,
another hoo-hoo-hoos,
and why does this duck
have a big beak, with
a pouch to dip for fish?
This duck is a helicopter,
dipping tiny beak in flowers.
They're all quacks
who only came to
march in my parade.

(Published in MuddyUm)

Don't Mix Milk and Meat

You want to mix it up, to box, to brawl.
I want to carve you into puzzle pieces,
fracture facial cream and gym-grown tone.
You want to milk me dry, cut through
the meat of what I mean. Nobody wins.
My words pour through you, puddle into buckets
to be left out for the cat. Your words congeal
into cudgel best served as a steak.
We can't live together on this plate of milk and meat.

(Published in Medusa's Kitchen)

Tree House

The tree and the house intertwined, grow together.
Doors are bored through by a gang of woodpeckers.
Room walls are branches that poke through the windows.
Ceilings are thatched with big leaves and old bird nests.
Sunlight and raindrops seep through every fissure.
Blue jays sing early in place of alarm clocks.
Squirrels bring me coffee and cupcakes on cracked plates.
They often are sloppy but I pay them peanuts.
They clean up their messes with big bushy tails.
Dust blows through tree rings and settles on flowers
that carpet the floors in bright purples and pinks.
Outside is inside and inside is out.

Splash

I didn't mean to turn all eyes
to my late soggy entrance.
When I left home, I was attired
in proper clothes for this affair.
But rain left puddles on the way
that called for me to jump in.
What joy to watch the drops fly up
in sheets of crystal water!
Now I drip across the floor.
I won't say I am sorry,
although I'll say I didn't plan
to make this kind of a splash.

(Published in Little Old Lady Comedy)

On the Other Side of Meno

Meno paused, packed up
the sweats, the chills, the flashes,
spurts of blood, the body morphing
into moody creature from a
feature no one wants to see.
She waved her ticket to Hawaii.
One way, I hope, I kicked
her ass goodbye and closed the door.
I didn't know she'd leave me
dry and fat and wide awake
with brittle bones to break,
and heart attacks to take me
to the grave.

She's such a bitch.

(Published in MasticadoresUSA)

Nesting Ground

I never fed a nest of nestlings,
never had a college fund to feed for
future when a body from my body
hated me enough to leave.
Who will grab the keys when I can't
drive and say it's time for me to stop?
Who will put me in a nest and feed
me when I lose my taste for food?

(Published in Contemplate)

Why I Don't Trust What I Remember

Memory is a leaky boat in a sink
in a kitchen with locks
but no doors and the keys
are buried in one of
the hundreds of boxes
of photos in the rest home
where my grandma
lost her name.

(Published in July 2023 Alien Buddha Zine)

My dreams

are mostly dead.
I want to revive them,
but the coffeemaker
in my dreams
has no cord
to plug into the wall.
There are no walls
in my dreams.
I want to build them,
but all I can find
are paper cups
filled with cold
coffee I couldn't make
without a cord.
Or a wall socket.
Or a wall.
My dreams are
mostly dead.

(Published in Spread)

I'm inside

the arrival of a woman
who walks through a door
of a house. All the doors
are the same. She walks
through a room like every
room in the house. She
crawls out a window, she
doesn't know which one, every
window in every room
is the same. She walks
around the house, a house
just like every house
on the block. I am inside
the arrival of a woman
who walks through
the door of the wrong
house. She is lost. I am
that woman.

Inspired by "Index" by Kell Connor

(Published in Contemplate)

Sleepless Demon

You are a wild child,
dancing to "Wake Up
Little Suzie" on my
head. In high heels.
Before sunrise, you
show your best moves.

Please turn on the coffee
before you get me
out of bed.

(Published in Medusa's Kitchen)

At least

Yellowstone hasn't erupted
and crisped me up, like
whatever it was in the
microwave that didn't come
to a good end. Tomorrow
the world may end. At least
the sky is clear and clean
and mystic blue. Tomorrow
the clouds will bloat and cry,
a crowd of women feeling fat
and sorry for eating all
the chocolate.

Things could be worse.

At this very moment,
I'm grateful.

I'm grateful.

(Published in The Piker Press)

Ode to road

maps, those that fold
into hidey holes that hold
the clutter someday useful,
if someday ever comes.
A road map, printed spider web
of lines that lead
to places no one goes,
with names so small,
they're written for a mouse.
(But mice use noses
they don't need directions
meant to turn the bravest
soul into a blubbering wreck.)
A road map, best to use
as napkin underneath
that hamburger you bought
at roadside rest, the one
that down the way
with no relief around,
will test your gut
and make you wish
you didn't leave
your home.

(Published in The Piker Press)

Anxious

The past wears
running shoes.
He catches up with me
as I slipslide to the future,
dragging my bag
of deceits.
The past is a mugger
with a bad suit
and a bad attitude.
The past has bad recall
and loves good stories.
He recites my wrongs,
even wrongs that
crossed my mind
but I forgot to do.
No wonder
I can't sleep.

(Published in The Piker Press)

Punctuation as a Blunt Instrument

Words pour out of my brain
so fast they slosh and froth
drain out the door to form
ice cubes sinking into the Arctic
Ocean to join the Iceberg Invitational
Open I don't have enough periods
to weigh me down and follow
their descent verify their demise
instead I ride a tilde through the thick
of thoughts they become a band
of bullies beating me with
explanation marks I hide
behind an ampersand scarfing
a caret cake I camouflage
myself as this poem arm myself
with commas and staple
myself to this page

W. S. Merwin's preface to his "Second Four Books of Poems,"
writes that he "relinquished punctuation," because he had begun
to feel that "it stapled the poems to the page."

(Published in Capella)

Incense of Absence

She lights the candles, incense
on the shrine to his departure.
Photographs and artwork
decorate the mantle,
as dancing light and sweet
aroma permeate the room.
She knows he won't return
but she peeks through
velvet curtains, soft and red
as heart-stained lifeblood
racing through the
tangled knots of adoration
beating time to footsteps
that will never walk again.

(Published in Lothlorien Poetry Journal)

Always

perfect, each hair in place,
facelift, hair dye, make-up
makes us wonder if you ever age.
Your clothes, all lace
and velvet, trimmed
with silk and satin.
Your favorite flowers, lilies,
clasped between your hands.
You're what I always
wished to be,

except that you are dead.

(Published in MasticadoresUSA)

I spilled red wine

on your white
angora sweater,
the one you
hung in my closet
when you were
out of town.
With my husband.

I'm so sorry

the stain
wasn't bigger.

(Published in The Gorko Gazette)

Sea shells

strewn across the sand,
a La Paz beach, so far
from seasons, far from
endless winter sea shells
stuffed in pockets,
tossed in buckets, here
they sit in blue glass
I bought long ago to store
us walking, you and I,
barefoot, browned, and daring
sea shell shards to rip
you from me, not to be,
a riptide of your own devising
dragged you off to sea.

Gently Used

I dropped my womb
off at Goodwill,
but they refused to take it.
Although it was gently used,
they said it was an oddity
that nobody would buy.

I told them it had served me well,
and could be used by others.
It could be a counter box
to store some day-old bread,
or gifted as a goblet,
or hold the ashes of somebody's
dear old dead friend Jed.

They nodded, said it
could indeed serve
many other uses.

They gave me a donation slip
and gently used a broom
to push me out the door
before I gave them
something else I'd used
they'd never seen before.

(Published in MasticadoresUSA and featured on My Bad Poetry
podcast)

Years after you die

I cling to you.
Your letters torn
and smudged with tears,
they crumble in my hands.
Your photos faded
from the sun, I barely
see you there.
Your favorite cup.
the pieces glued,
I cannot throw it out.
I won't believe
that I can grow
away from memories.

(Published in The Wind Phone)

Thought is a caterpillar

wiggling down the spine,
making a left into the mouth,
and fluttering out as a word butterfly.

Sometimes, it turns too soon
and slides down the nose.
Then, it's just snot.

(Published in Five Fleas and featured in My Bad Poetry podcast)

She opened her mouth

and swallowed a bird.
She spit out feathers
instead of words.

(Published in Five Fleas)

Junk Love

She buried him in love
to fill her empty heart.
She brought home
feral felines,
puppies found
in garbage bins,
shadeless lamps and
soiled sweats and
moldy bread,
whatever she could find.
Her love was blind,
rejected junk and child
were the same to her.
Discards piled higher, faster,
than he could toss them out.
Knowing it would never end,
he walked away and left her
to be buried in her trash.

(Published in MasticadoresIndia)

Bad Santa

Life crawls down
the chimney at night,
empties my closet
of childhood,
and leaves me

this wrinkled old body.

(Published in The Gorko Gazette)

She paints her face

with cold cream and grief.
She chooses to forget
his deep-freeze feelings,
the icy silence sleeping
in the space between them.
She holds their wedding picture,
holds the pledge of lifetime love,
regardless of the bruises
on her heart.

(Published in Medusa's Kitchen)

My pelvis wants to be Elvis

on The Ed Sullivan Show, you know,
I want to be that cutie who shakes her booty
while Elvis bumps and grinds. Who minds
gyrating hips and snarling lips?
The truth be said, my darling Ed,
the rest of me wants to be

in bed.

(Published in Medusa's Kitchen)